Play Trumpet Today! Songbook

Featuring 10 Pop & Movie Favorites!

ISBN 0-634-02896-0

HAL•LEONARD®
CORPORATION

7777 W. BLUEMOUND RD. P.O. BOX 13819 MILWAUKEE, WI 53213

Visit Hal Leonard Online at
www.halleonard.com

Introduction

Welcome to the *Trumpet Songbook*. This book includes several well-known pop and movie favorites, and is intended for the beginner to intermediate player.

The ten songs in this book are coordinated with the skills introduced throughout levels one and two of the method, *Play Trumpet Today!*

Contents

About the CD

A recording of each song in the book is included on the CD, so you can hear how it sounds and play along when you're ready. Each example is preceded by one measure of "clicks" to indicate the tempo and meter. Pan right to hear the solo part emphasized. Pan left to hear the accompaniment emphasized.

Track 1

Forrest Gump–Main Title
(Feather Theme)
from the Paramount Motion Picture FORREST GUMP

TRUMPET

Music by ALAN SILVESTRI

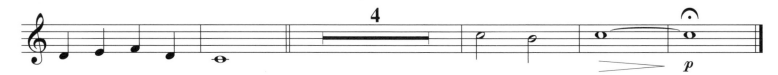

We Will Rock You

Track 2

TRUMPET

Words and Music by BRIAN MAY

Chariots Of Fire

from CHARIOTS OF FIRE

Music by VANGELIS

Track 3

TRUMPET

Rock & Roll–Part II

Track 4

(The Hey Song)

TRUMPET

Words and Music by
MIKE LEANDER and GARY GLITTER

Steady Rock Shuffle

Track 5

Smoke On The Water

TRUMPET

Words and Music by RITCHIE BLACKMORE, IAN GILLAN,
ROGER GLOVER, JON LORD and IAN PAICE

Heavy Rock

Play 3rd and 4th times only

Yesterday

Track 6

TRUMPET

Words and Music by
JOHN LENNON and PAUL McCARTNEY

Gently

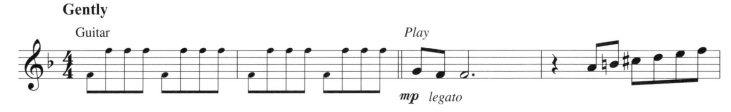

Twist And Shout

Track 7

TRUMPET

Words and Music by
BERT RUSSELL and PHIL MEDLEY

Driving 60's Rock

Star Trek®– The Motion Picture

Theme from the Paramount Picture STAR TREK: THE MOTION PICTURE

Track 8

TRUMPET

Music by JERRY GOLDSMITH

Track 9

You've Got A Friend In Me

from Walt Disney's TOY STORY

TRUMPET

Music and Lyrics by RANDY NEWMAN

Raiders March

from the Paramount Motion Picture
RAIDERS OF THE LOST ARK

Track 10

TRUMPET

By JOHN WILLIAMS

Play Trumpet Today!

The Ultimate Self-Teaching Method's Level 1

Play Trumpet Today!
A Complete Guide to the Basics

Teacher on CD • 73 Demo Tracks

HAL•LEONARD®

The Ultimate Self-Teaching Method

This series provides a complete guide to the basics with quality instruction, terrific songs, and a professional-quality CD with each book. It can be used by students who want to teach themselves, or by teachers for private or group instruction. Simply follow the tips and lessons in the book as you listen to the teacher on the CD.

Level One

Your first guide to the basics includes over 70 songs and examples; how to assemble & care for the instrument; producing a sound; reading music notation and rhythms; fingering chart; glossary of musical terms.

00842052 Book/CD Pack $9.95

Level Two

Level two includes over 70 songs and examples; review of assembly & instrument care; more great music; more new notes, keys, and rhythms; fingering chart; glossary of musical terms.

00842053 Book/CD Pack $9.95

Songbook

This great supplement lets students play 10 pop and movie favorites with the accompanying CD. Songs include: Forrest Gump-Main Title • We Will Rock You • Chariots Of Fire • Rock & Roll-Part II (The Hey Song) • Smoke On The Water • Yesterday • Twist And Shout • Star Trek®-The Motion Picture • You've Got A Friend In Me • Raiders March.

00842054 Book/CD Pack $12.95

FOR MORE INFORMATION, SEE YOUR LOCAL MUSIC DEALER, OR WRITE TO:

HAL•LEONARD®
CORPORATION

7777 W. BLUEMOUND RD. P.O. BOX 13819 MILWAUKEE, WI 53213